ERIN,

YOU'RE A BEAUTIFUL RED
ROSE!

BE BOLD!
BE OPEN!
BE STRONG!

YOU HAVE A BUTTERFLY IN
TRAINING! TEACH
HIM TO:

FLY HIGH!
FLY STRONG!
FLY BRAVE!

BEST WISHES,
John Rhie
찬 기

The Rose

And

The Butterfly

Written by
John Kim
Illustrated by
Mallory Steele

To my parents: my father, Chong Pae Kim, and my mother, Tae Hui Kim, for having the courage and making the sacrifice to come to the United States, from Korea, to give a better life for me and my siblings (Gina Yong-Chu Kim Lammers, Chong Su Kim, and Kristy Yong Su Kim Lee). To my son, Jameson Conor Kim, who inspires me everyday. To Frank Faris for being my Aikido teacher, my counsel, and my friend for over 20 years. To Myrna Siegel Duthu for being a loyal friend and advisor for 20 years. To my brother-in law Col. Carl Lammers, USMC (Ret.) who has always been there for me. To the kind and gracious Inessa Monique Vitko, her kindness and graciousness can be seen through her running charity, Team J and I- with her running partner, Jennifer Heitz, for the Leukemia and Lymphoma Society. To Elizabeth Bergeron, Brad Bundy, Dawn Benny-Estep, Clare Fertitta Seibert, and Robert A. Gardenghi for their support, advice, and friendship on all aspects of this book. To Alice Loh, Russell King, and Josie Coppolino for their advice on early iterations of some illustrations. To Katya Merclyakova for helping in fine tuning some of the layout. To Katie Eltz for her help. To Celia Wrisk, mother to Mathew, Bernie, Valerie Wrisk-Gray, and Gregory- I went to Catonsville High School with all of them, for her help in editing this book.

Deep in the forest grew an angry, short, closed White Rose.

The White Rose tried to fight against the Wind's gentle push. The Wind always proved too strong.

On the floor of the forest was a young, innocent Caterpillar, joyfully, going on its way. Not looking where it was going, it bumped into the White Rose.

The White Rose looked down, with anger, and said, "WATCH where you are going!" It startled the Caterpillar.

The Caterpillar apologized then quickly went on its way. The White Rose stood there fuming. It was mad at the Caterpillar for not looking at where it was going.

Again, the Caterpillar bumped into the White Rose. It braced itself for mean words but only saw the wilted leaves of the White Rose.

The Caterpillar asked, "What is wrong?"

The White Rose replied, "I am sad because you are able to walk around while I am forced to live where I am planted."

The Caterpillar said, "I may be able to walk around but I can only see things from the ground. You have a much better view than I do. In time you will be able to see the top of the forest."

The White Rose said, "I am not that much taller than you. I have never thought of it that way."

That spring day a friendship was born. Often, the Caterpillar would come by; staying longer with each visit. As time passed, the White Rose did not fight the Wind as much and began to open up.

One day, the Caterpillar came to the same spot that it had visited many times before. It looked to the left, to the right, up and down but did not see the White Rose.

What the Caterpillar did see was a pretty, tall, open Pink Rose.

The Caterpillar asked, "Excuse me, please, have you seen my friend, the White Rose?"

The Pink Rose replied, "My Caterpillar friend, I have not moved. I was once the White Rose. With your love and friendship, you have taught me to open and show color. For that great gift, thank you."

The Caterpillar said, "It will soon be time for me to go into my chrysalis. May I attach myself to you, please?"

The Pink Rose said. "It would be an honor."

Not being able to move around the Caterpillar swung its chrysalis back and forth, bumping into the same place on the Pink Rose, hurting it.

The Pink Rose asked, "Why do you keep trying to move, when you know you can't?"

The Caterpillar replied, "I am so used to moving around that being held to one place bothers me."

The Pink Rose said, "Sometimes in life you must be still in order to change."

With much effort the Caterpillar was able to remain still.

One spring day, a beautiful Butterfly fell from its chrysalis. Tripping over its wings, it tried to embrace its new form. The Butterfly slowly got used to its Butterfly self.

The Butterfly tried to find its friend the Pink Rose. It did not see the Pink Rose but a beautiful, tall, fully open Red Rose. The Butterfly stood there with its mouth open, not breathing or speaking, just staring.

The Butterfly asked, "Excuse me, please, have you seen my friend, the Pink Rose?"

The Red Rose replied, "My Butterfly friend, I have not moved. I was once the Pink Rose. With your love and friendship, I have found my true color and opened my petals fully to the world."

"Before I fought the Wind; I now dance with the Wind. Before I was short and closed; I am now tall and open to the world. You have allowed me to grow and blossom where I am planted. The view of the forest is more wonderful than I could have dreamed. In me you saw a seed of potential. You showered it with love. Now I am filled with endless hope."

The Red Rose said, "You, my friend, have also changed; you have beautiful wings."

The Butterfly, looking at its wings, asked, "What am I supposed to do with these 'wings' as you call them?"

The Red Rose replied, "They are for you to fly!"

The Butterfly took a few steps, flew about a foot, then hit the ground. It tried to fly but could not.

The Butterfly said, "I am scared."

The Red Rose said, "My friend, you must try with all your might. You were made to fly and fly you must. I will encourage you with all the love that I can send to you."

The Butterfly flew short distances at first. With encouragement from the Red Rose, it flew higher and higher.

With its new flying ability, the Butterfly quickly flew back to the Red Rose.

The Butterfly said, "Thank you for giving me the courage to fly!"

The Red Rose said, "Thank you for giving me the courage to reach heights I never thought that I could and open myself to the world!"

Nestling the Butterfly in its petals, the Red Rose said:

"Welcome home!"

Love is the great transformer!

Love transforms all who touch and are touched by it. May someone give you the courage and encouragement to discover the Red Rose or the Butterfly in all of us.

Made in the USA
Middletown, DE
30 July 2015